Grade 2½

As recorded by BTS

Butter

Words and Music by Jenna Andrews, Stephen Kirk, Sebastian Garcia,
Robert Grimaldi, Ron Perry, Alex Bilowitz and Kim Nam-Joon
Arranged by Michael Story

--- **INSTRUMENTATION** ---

1	Full Score
8	Violin I
8	Violin II
5	Violin III (Viola 𝄞)
5	Viola
5	Cello
5	String Bass
2	Drumset
2	Percussion
	(Tambourine, Tom-Toms [2])

NOTES TO THE CONDUCTOR

This catchy tune from the band BTS occupied the #1 spot for many weeks in 2021. The dotted-eighth/sixteenth-tied-to-an-eighth/eighth rhythm is utilized throughout the arrangement. Introduce or reinforce this rhythm in your warmup routine, stressing rhythmic accuracy and ensemble precision.

The staccato quarter notes should be played in the middle of the bow on the string with a martelé bow stroke. The staccato eighth notes should be played on the string as well, but in the lower third of the bow.

There are easy drumset and percussion parts included—both are totally optional. The 1st violin part in measures 34–37 can be performed either as a solo or by the section.

I hope you and your ensemble enjoy *Butter*!

Michael Story

smartmusic.

Power Your Teaching

NOTE FROM THE EDITOR

In orchestral music, there are many editorial markings that are open for interpretation. In an effort to maintain consistency and clarity you may find some of these markings in this piece. In general, markings for fingerings, bowing patterns, and other items will only be marked with their initial appearance. For a more detailed explanation of our editorial markings, please download the free PDF at www.alfred.com/stringeditorial.

X	–	,	(♭), (♯), (♮)	⊓ ⊓ *or* V V
extended position	shift	bow lift/reset	high or low fingerings	hooked bowings

Belwin ORCHESTRA
a division of Alfred

As recorded by BTS

Butter

FULL SCORE
Duration - 1:55

Words and Music by Jenna Andrews,
Stephen Kirk, Sebastian Garcia,
Robert Grimaldi, Ron Perry,
Alex Bilowitz and Kim Nam-Joon
Arranged by Michael Story

49445S

*Purchase a full-length
performance recording!*
alfred.com/downloads